Dharma seasoned
rhythm rhyme and reason.

No citations for scholarly interpretation,
just irreverently serious word cumulations,
to teach, entertain, light bulbs at mind stations.

Best for clever seekers
wearing open laugh sneakers.

mitch

Thank you so much for
the gift of your feedback
and being!

Fuel for this fire
of creativity.

Warmest wishes
Eugeo :)

4

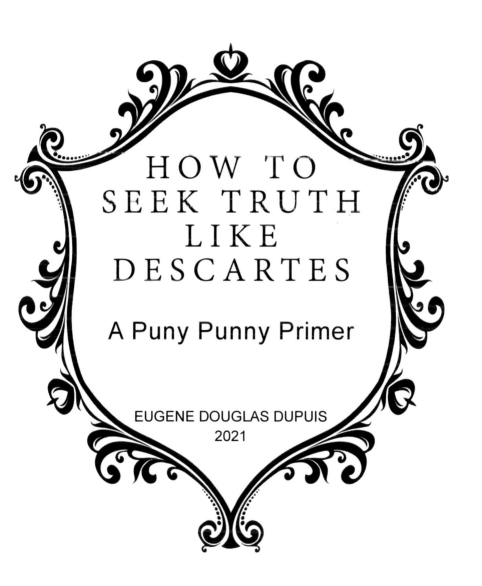

HOW TO SEEK TRUTH LIKE DESCARTES

A Puny Punny Primer

EUGENE DOUGLAS DUPUIS
2021

Whatʼs waiting where

Dew worms and donuts

Do contemplate one Meditation a day.
Do not rush wisdom or play.

Meditation
is contemplation.
Single pointed concentration.

Flow. The Zone. Time standing still.
Tranquil trail to truth when you empty the till.

Don't try to understand meaning.
Nothing has intrinsic meaning.
Meaning to you, is the meaning you give it.
Always, all ways, all the time.

God talk here.
God's what you say God is. If you do.
Supreme creator for Descartes.
Good Old Dharma for Dupuis.
Whatever wonder works for ewe's ok.
Best if All True Istic.

Don't get stuck.
No scratch in this vinyl.
Smooth move into the groove.

Like Descartes. please pause after each chapter.
Single-pointedly contemplate
what's there in the air.

You can practice single pointed concentration
to improve your contemplation.
Use your breath as an anchor
to the present situation.

Use your breath to practice with me now.
You might say wow or holy cow.
It's simple, here's how.
Read what's below,
then do it now.

Close your eyes. Take a long slow breath.
Breathe in through your nose real slow.
Sense the tickle of cool air in your nostrils.

Breathe out through your lips real slow.
All the way out. To the very end.
Sense the current of your breath,
taking tension out with it.

Notice distractions as they appear,
Gently return to attend breath.

No trying. No judgment. No right. No wrong.
It's just practice.

This practice improves contemplation
and appreciation of life.

Even one breath counts.

Please, take one now.

10

Dribble on Descartes

1641. Everyone West knew, all that was true,
was from bible and wise Greeks that once grew.
Logic and argument only truth proof from that pew.

Along came Frenchie René. Found a better way.
Showed those guys good. It wasn't what they say.
What everyone knew, was found untrue.
Including most of what's seen or believed.

Like Socrates, he drank the divine duty drink
that drove both to change how people think.

Meditations was his search for truth through first peas of knowledge.
Outside of math, he established steps in a path,
that always found truth and a laugh.
An influential text, tall as a giraffe.

Our five senses deceive, hold us in a bind.
Beliefs from senses mostly made up by our mind.
Flush crappy senses that keep us truth blind.

Go to sense six, a new method for a minute.
Open universe size window in a space they call infinite.
Beyond the intellect.

Truth and God await self-discovery,
No logic or argument.

It was revolutionary.

Dribble on Dupuis

Searching for essence since sixteen.
Teachers, travels and a big magazine.

27himalayandays, three alone in a cave.
Buddhist and Bodhisattva vows came.

Studied Descartes' Meditations at York.
Wrote a verse connecting concepts, like knife and fork.
Couldn't stop at one. Learned and had fun.
Captured ideas, essence,
then went on a pun run.

Descartes' smugly aloof, but he's no goof.
Wisdom in here, and it's right through the roof.

Wisdom helps others without fail.
So, to make a difference at scale.
Outside a big box, no bail pail,
Dupuis channels this book and sets sail.

Ten days up the channel,
three hundred polishing the deck.

It's a quirky creative expression,
for your consideration and inspiration.

Wishfully it makes a difference.

RENATI
DES-CARTES,
MEDITATIONES
DE PRIMA
PHILOSOPHIA,
IN QVA DEI EXISTENTIA
ET ANIMÆ IMMORTALITAS
DEMONSTRATVR.

PARISIIS,
Apud MICHAELEM SOLY, viâ Iacobeâ, sub
signo Phœnicis.

M. DC. XLI.

Cùm Priuilegio, & Approbatione Doctorum.

Meditation I
infinite sphere of the doubtful.

I don't believe now,
much I believed when younger.
Just ain't true I would die from hunger.

Older now. May be wiser.
But never too long in the tooth to find truth.
If I want that booth.
What if it's uncouth?

Can I know absolute,
as an absolutely finite being?
Doesn't sound promising.

Do I want tough task of truth finding?
What if it's deep and darkly blinding?

Of what alone can I be sure?
On what to build a case,
to find first principles of knowledge,
from which all else to base?

Still not sure math's aim is true.
Math method may miss this mark.
We need to analyze, not synthesize,
to light the deep and dark.

I'll conduct a peppermint experiment
with thought.

Our senses do deceive.
On these we need disbelieve.
Doubt 'till truth perceived.
Banish five sense prejudice.

Near infinite delusions need poof without pout.
Bring in the closer, Hyperbolic Doubt.
The truth brush to clean them all out.

With a sliver of unreasonable doubt that it's real,
I'll deny every roof, tooth, proof and truth.
Deny. Defy. Crucify. Goodbye fry. Beliefs will die.

I'm always deceived in what's perceived.
Don't believe all I think true cheese.
Banish all beliefs before sunset's tease.

Things in dreams seem real, but nope.
Mind creates seemingly real rope. Real dope.

But everything real hatched,
has something real attached.

Math is left alone, but may be a no.
Why would I be deceived? I don't know.
To move on, I'll pretend Evil Genius breath blows.

Everything is gone now.
I'm naked. Doubt stripped bare.
I am now nothing. Nothing is there.
Except infinite space nestling truth in its care.

Let's pause now. Imbed what's found in the air.
Sense-six this new thing nothingness.

Close your eyes. Take a few deep, slow breaths.
Cool air in tickles your nostrils.
Tension flows out slowly through lips.

Gently notice distractions.
Return to breath.

No trying allowed. No judgement.
Gentle single-pointed concentration
on the nothingness in your breath.

This is where ideas from nowhere come from.

Practice while you dine,
or listen to chimes,
or anytime
is fine.

* Graduation registry for Descartes at the University of Poitiers, 1616 from Le Prytanee Militaire, Public Domain,

Meditation II
existence. nature of mind and body.

Drowning in oceans of doubt.
Hard work focusing on truth.
Certainly hard, to find anything certain,
if anything certainly is.

Persuaded there's nothing in memory,
senses or fictions of mind.
Is there anything, anywhere,
doubtless to find?

Is there a me who wonders
about pie in the eye?
Or does God place wonder in this guy?

Flesh nor figure, place nor space,
Senses neither win truth's race.

Mind knows better than senses.
Knows wax whether candle, puddle or stamp.

Wait a minute!
What of thinking?

Doubt snot there anywhere.
Thought's the answer, no despair.

Thought is definitely me.

I know I exist, because I think, that alone is certain.
But what is thought behind that curtain?

Include deception and persuasion
in a galaxy of thought in action.
All of it inseparable from me.

I clearly know I've been deceived.
Know I was persuaded.
This is proof I must exist.
Neither these doubt jaded.

Cogito, ergo sum.
I think therefore I am.
That's worth a damn.
Grand slam!

Do I now doubt I am human?
Or what human is?
Two more cans of focus-fizz.

Mind might be human essence.
Mind is everywhere,
Delivers clear and distinct clarity,
when truth's really, actually there.

Clear and distinct intuition.
Value this truthful vision.
Another one over the fence!

Now what of I's existence?
Empty of inherent, independent existence?
Extension of omnipotent?

Meditation II
existence. nature of mind and body.

Drowning in oceans of doubt.
Hard work focusing on truth.
Certainly hard, to find anything certain,
if anything certainly is.

Persuaded there's nothing in memory,
senses or fictions of mind.
Is there anything, anywhere,
doubtless to find?

Is there a me who wonders
about pie in the eye?
Or does God place wonder in this guy?

Flesh nor figure, place nor space,
Senses neither win truth's race.

Mind knows better than senses.
Knows wax whether candle, puddle or stamp.

Wait a minute!
What of thinking?

Doubt snot there anywhere.
Thought's the answer, no despair.

Thought is definitely me.

I know I exist, because I think, that alone is certain.
But what is thought behind that curtain?

RENATUS DESCARTES, NOBIL. GALL. PERRONI DOM. SUMMUS MATHEM. ET PHILO

Talis erat vultu NATURÆ FILIUS: *unus Assignansq; fuis quavis miracula causâ*
Qui Menti in Matris viscera pandit iter. Miraculum reliquum solus in orbe fuit.

* Descartes at work. Public Domain,.wikimedia.org

Meditation III
perception deception. ideas. God proof.

A thing that thinks about zillions of things.
Things apart, but a part of me.

What else is? Can truth tell I?
Only with clarity of my inner eye.
But what persuaded me, a thinking thing, says hi?

I'm a perfect perception, perceived clear and distinct.
What is the nature of "I am a thing which thinks"?

It's not eternally, terminally untrustworthy,
silly putty senses.

Must be in the thought itself.
I'll be an elf, reflect myself
on what persuades me.

My existence is clean.
No dirty doubt in that bubble bath.
Math is distinct too, but no good for this path.

Knowing God is through intuition,
impossibly perceived in five sense condition.

So, I hesitate to generalize, but set a general rule.
Clear is true, I'm no fool. Like the Golden Rule.

But what see I, that fooled me fore?
That seemed so real, but holds no more?
Believed I perceived, perceived like a boor.

Three percent is what I really see.
The rest my mind makes up to be,
as an idea.

Memories can't be trusted as true,
just a drama I create from ideas past due.

Ideas are images of things, shadows at best.
Cloudy and obscure, when put to the test.
Represent nothing as some kind of pest.

Idea of a tree needs a tree to be.

But idea of God is independent.
Only God could put God's idea there.
This is Proof One, God's in the air.

But unfortunately,
This proof goes poof when I'm distracted.

No absolute truth in any proof anyway.
Proof's not given; it's taken. Often mistaken.
Mere beacons of logic, lighting trails taken
to mountains of knowledge and bacon.

Even false proofs are used for direction.
NASA using flat earth gets ship to moon station.

Nothing to do but try proof number two.
Can I, who has the idea of God,
exist if God doesn't?

Something cannot come from nothing,
More perfect cannot come from less.

Imperfect me, nothing more perfect than He.
This idea placed by God I see.

To think myself finite while denying the infinite.
Impossible as spin-it to win-it.

Logically inseparable. The infinite exists. Forever.

Proof Two of God taken.
A better beacon bonbon,
moistening lips that are thirsty for truth.

I have idea of God. I have idea of me
How are these connected,
Such that divided they cannot be?

What necessary connection exists
like motion and duration?
I meditate not argue,
open in contemplation.

I enter the place that God and I share.
Nothing but space, in infinite air.

A seismic electric sensation appears.
Joyous, giant, big sobbing tears.

It's so real it's unreal.

We're one current, God and me be.
God's art and idea imprinted in me,
Picasso's technique in painting of a pea.
Clear and distinct I see.

In the aftermath of this revelation.
Now knowing God, I take blissful reflection.
Contemplate at leisure, ultimate perfection.

Pause now. Close your eyes. Breathe slow and deep.
Cool air in tickles nostrils. Out breath carries tension.
Gently notice distracting thoughts. Return to breath

Float in your breath, sensing the wonder of God,
or anything else wonderful.

Contemplate. Admire.
Adore divine attributes.

Bask in the glory, if glory appears.
No trying. No judgement.
It's all good whatever.

Similar meditations, less perfect than this,
still cause the greatest satisfactions.

* The house where René Descartes was born, le haye en tourene.

28

Meditation IV
true and false. judgement. imperfection.

We know little for certain of sensory things.
Certainly, more certain we know existence and God.
Better than bumps in a bog.

See them rice crispy clear,
Can't prevent from knowing true.
A perfect God exists, created me and you.

No room for err in thoughts of God.
Just saturation in perfection confection,
from clear and distinct intelligence.

I mess up a lot. Make mistakes.
Still think God is there.
Inseparable. A perfect pear.
As mountain is to valley air.

I judge all else from what I think I know,
then act free willy-nilly.

When Willy's will is wider than understanding,
err is powerfully put to abuse.

Error in judgement's actions
testify to glaring imperfections.

God makes us imperfect,
giving us this rampant room to err.
What freak in logic's hiding there?

Nature and I so feeble. God so immense.
No denying, what I see won't make sense.

What don't work for me, is best for eternity.
Perfect is not what was meant to be.
Universal perfection results from my lack.

May be the key, to a life that's bright,
is living imperfectly with delight.

Pause now. Ponder what's present.

Close your eyes. Take three slow breaths.
Cool air in tickles nostrils. Outbreath carries tension.
Gently notice distracting thoughts. Return to breath.

Dwell in your breath.
Ask about judgement.

Be a contemplation sleuth.
How might it colour your truth?

Notice distractions, gently return to breath.
Stay with it. Be patient.
Ponder what comes up,
if anything.

Practice this contemplation for wisdom.

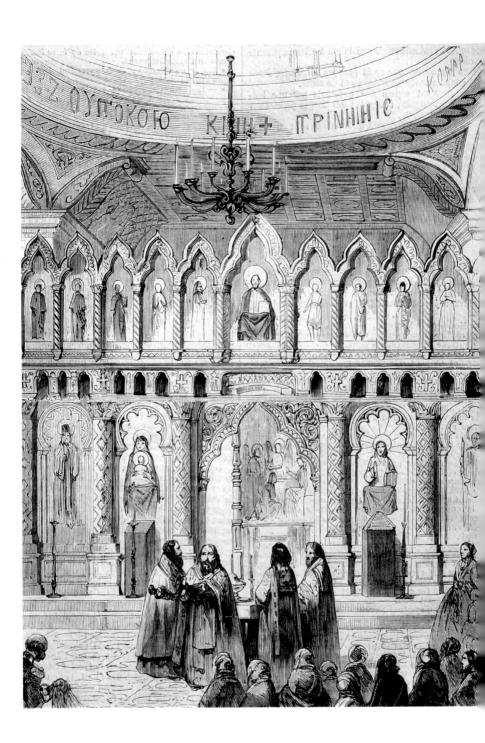

Meditation V
essence. clarity. truth

I know not what's certain or real.
Except certainty of God's real deal

What objects I conceive to be,
that exist outside of me,
are clear and distinct?

Flush the rest down the kitchen sink.

Real ideas come from thought.
Like all I am belongs,
and figures oblong that tag along.

My prospecting mind discovers distinct,
from what was already there.

I don't invent a triangle from nowhere.

Yet imagining is not understanding or truth.

Real are horses and wings.
I can imagine a horse with wings.
But winged horses aren't things.

I see God complete.
No options found.
Every perfection abounds.

Mind is not body, but inseparably linked,
More inseparable than pretty and pink.

All that is true is something.
All I know clearly is true.
No holding back truth.
When clearly conceived,
in it's due.

Forcefully propelled, I see God at the table
infinite and unchangeable.

It's a powerful persuasion position
they call psychological disposition.

From a good God that is,
From which all I am depends,
Clarity is true blue.
Nothing to defend to my friend.

Pause now. Imbed deeply what's found new.
First Phil Clarity, clear and distinct taken true.

Close your eyes. Take three slow breaths.
Cool air in tickles nostrils. Out breath carries tension
Gently notice distracting thoughts. Return to breath

Float in your breath for a bit longer.
Ask about clear and distinct for you.

Ponder thoughts on clarity as they arise.
How do you know that you know clearly?
What is clear and distinct to you,

Notice distractions.
Gently return to attend breath.

No trying. No judgement.
No right. No wrong.

Practice this contemplation
to see more clearly more often.

Meditation VI (a)
material existence. imagination. unreality.

You've got good patience, if you're still here.
Ride's almost over. End and essence seem near.
Pick up a pointer. Trudge on to truth.

I'm still pondering material things.
Are all things perceived clear true?
Like math and you?

God creates everything, perceived clearly so.
Mind of confusion is where all the rest go.

Imagination armed with knowledge
persuades us material things are real.

Effort is needed to imagine.
Imagination is not needed for me.
I must depend on something
completely different to be.

What exists for intellect and I to meet?
What joins mind, to imagine joined concrete?

Imagine no mind for body at all.
Only acceptance of fire and fall.
There'd be no idea of thirst or pain Et al.

Imagination finds the body familiar.
If the body is true, it perceives or conceives,
by itself or with senses, what's real.
That's a mouthful of meaningful.

Possibly probable the body is true
Clear and distinct, probably not.

Body parts, others, emotions,
pleasure, pain, hunger and thirst.
Lively and clear, appear not from mind,
but from somewhere different first.

As I'm pushed to perceive what's present.
idea of object is different from real.

My only knowledge of body,
is what body's idea itself gave me.
That's good gravy.

Ideas form of myself, sense sans reason.
Clear as soggy foggy lenses.

I can't believe I was once persuaded
by all ideas from fab five senses.

Not just outside, but inside me too.
Phantom pains in missing limbs.
That's not real. That won't do.

I see stick as a snake.
Best not to make sense out of senses.

I've a passive perception for particles,
and propensity to produce ideas not me.
Dew, however, objectively contains,
what my eye actually sees to be.

Hunger causes me to eat, thirst to drink,
pain to sadness, pleasure to joy.

Sweet dreams of sunshine
seep inside sleeping me.
Also live inside me,
when awake I seem to be.

Me, core, a thinking thing.
Body extended unthinking.
Clearly seen different but linking.

Entangled birds of a feather.
Caught, in a caged cot, together.

Indivisible invisible mind is one.
Visible divisible body is more.
Mind is different than body.
Another answer at the Knowledge door.

I see me complete, clear and distinct.

Don't need imagining or feeling.
Those two are outside of me,
from an Other intelligent host being.

As God not deceives, I believe I've received
a means to know ultimate truth.
What seems real is not always so.
How uncouth.

Let's pause now. Imbed what we've found new.

Close your eyes. Take three slow breaths.
Cool air in tickles nostrils. Out breath carries tension.
Gently notice distracting thoughts. Return to breath

Then float in your breath.
Ask about material existence,
and what lies beyond it.

Or ponder anything else that's there.

Gently notice distracting thoughts.
Return to your breath.
No trying.

This contemplation has you see beyond.

Meditation VI (b)
nature. truth. no end.

Some truth contained in nature.
Body paired with pain. Thirst for water.
Yet heat needn't be here to be hot.
Mind can do that solo, no matter.

But why my dry throat from tiny thirst?
Shouldn't I be dying of thirst first?
It's all very confusing. Doesn't make sense.
Logic's not fixing this broken fence.

Mind lodged in body appear as one.
Perfectly paired natural deceivers.

God could make brain without pain.
Wouldn't conserve me Tarzan or you Jane.
Conservation's not in the perfection lane.

Nature's omniscient, that doesn't astonish.
My unlimited limits can't see perfect finish.

Deceit is rampant. It's all repugnant,
Time to meet with my maker sublime.
God greets me, tunes me like clockwork
to once again hold perfect time.

Returned to the me I was conceived to be.

Now, let's get off the pot. Rubber hit the road.
Urge of action obliges decision,
before rural retreat in contemplation.

Hence, I must now conclude fair.
Life sucks with err.

We're misled by all but the clear and distinct.
Drain the rest down the kitchen sink.

Flush hyperbole down the toilet bowl.
Evil Genius, throw in the towel.
I'm so relieved I could howl.

No more worry of fear or falsity.
Thankfully sleep and wake are different.
I need some of the first.

No decision to make about God.
Clear and distinct, God just is. Intuitively.
Perfect. Created me, who's perfect two,
The clear and distinct is true too.

Now comes vacation.
A more peaceful contemplation.
With nature alone, in its natural formation.

Please pause frequently. Close your eyes.
Take a few deep slow breaths.

Cool breath in tickles nostrils.
Slow out breath takes tension with it.
Notice distractions. Return to breath.

Repeat

No end

BONUS
CONTENT

BIBLIOTHÈQUE DES TEXTES PHILOSOPHIQUES

DIRECTEUR : HENRI GOUHIER

RENÉ DESCARTES

REGULÆ

AD DIRECTIONEM

INGENII

TEXTE DE L'ÉDITION ADAM ET TANNERY

NOTICE PAR HENRI GOUHIER

LIBRAIRIE PHILOSOPHIQUE J. VRIN

* Regulae cover: Source Librairie Philosophique J. Vrin

Regulae
Descartes' rules for direction of the mind.

First four rules establish methods of math.
The rest are adaptations for wisdom's path.
Here's a snippet, not a synopsis,
a sliver of a skim, to ponder in your bath.

1. *Acquire wisdom*
    Proceed with wisdom's end in mind.
    Use sound and correct judgement
    on all matters before you.
    Explore beyond scholarly questions.

2. *Focus on what you know*
    Don't bite off more than you can chew.
    Ask for help where you're not strong,
    or your song won't be long for John.

3. *Be 100% certain*
    Only two tools needed for this certain season.
    Conceive by intuitive light of reason,
    or deduce from known principles with certainty.

4. *Systemize and analyze*
    Four score, to get more smores,
    determine rules and steps that always score more.
    Work hard. Don't assume what's true about rings.
    Exhaust near infinite considerations.

5. ***One step at a time***
   Exhaustively examine the intuitively understood.
   The absolutely simple steps first.
   Proceed only when these are clear.
   Transform large, complicated leaps
   into multiple, small, simple steps.

6. ***Study and organize the facts***
   Penetrate your insight on the minutest of facts.
   What is simple, pure and absolute within its shack?
   What is most relative and dependent on Jack?
   What do you know? What do you need to know?

7. ***Be here, now***
   Give your utmost, full, uninterrupted attention
   to what's here now, at this station.
   Use continuous, methodical, movement of mind.
   Visualize and memorize order and connections.

8. ***Let go***
   Don't drown in a puddle of ignorance.
   Go no further than what you intuitively understand.
   Be honest, not overconfident, in the land of sand.
   Nature of people or problems may prevent progress.
   If so, move on and let go.

9. ***Concentrate single-pointedly***
Clear your time and mind.
Contemplate individually, at length, everything,
until truth appears clear and distinct for each.

10. ***Blaze a trail***
Discover truth and reason by our own efforts
to yield the highest intellectual satisfaction.
Study what others don't.
Go your own way.
Break the rules.

11. ***See the big picture***
Apply continuous and uninterrupted attention
on the complete chain of logic.
Contemplate the relationships of facts and steps.
Grasp together distinctly, a number of propositions,
so far as possible, at the same time.

12. ***Be extrasensory***
Tap into your creative spiritual power
to perceive truth, clear and distinct.
Use imagination to perceive
what understanding misses.
Sense how your truths compare to others'.

RENÉ DESCARTES

MEDITATIONS
ON
FIRST PHILOSOPHY

*A new edition, edited and
with an introduction
by Stanley Tweyman*

---

* Cover of René Descartes'; Meditations on First Philosophy;
the text used as source and inspiration for these verses.

Meditations on the First Philosophy in which the Existence of God and the Distinction Between Mind and Body are Demonstrated[1]

Rid yourself of sensory messages *method of Hyperbolic Doubt* *Clear your mind*

MEDITATION I

Of the things which may be brought within the sphere of the doubtful

It is now some years since I detected how many were the false beliefs that I had from my earliest youth admitted as true, and how doubtful was everything I had since constructed on this basis, and from that time I was convinced that I must once for all seriously undertake to rid myself of all the opinions which I had formerly accepted, and commence to build anew from the foundation, if I wanted to establish any firm and permanent structure in the sciences. But as this enterprise appeared to be a very great one, I waited until I had attained an age so mature that I could not hope that at any later date I should be better fitted to execute my design. This reason caused me to delay so long that I should feel that I was doing wrong were I to occupy in deliberation the time that yet remains to me for action. To-day, then, since very opportunely for the plan I have in view I have delivered my mind from every care [and am happily agitated by no passions] and since I have procured for myself an assured leisure in a peaceable retirement, I shall at last

grew / wise *open self to all possible* *start fresh from what is solid*

Now is the start

---

[1] In place of this long title at the head of the page the first Edition had immediately after the Synopsis, and on the same page 7, simply "First Meditation." (Adam's Edition.)

---

* Author's musings from René Descartes'; Meditations on First Philosophy; a new edition, edited and with an introduction by Stanley Tweyman.

50

seriously and freely address myself to the general upheaval of all my former opinions.

Now for this object it is not necessary that I should show that all of these are false — I shall perhaps never arrive at this end. But inasmuch as reason already persuades me that I ought no less carefully to withhold my assent from matters which are not entirely certain and indubitable than from those which appear to me manifestly to be false, if I am able to find in each one some reason to doubt, this will suffice to justify my rejecting the whole. And for that end it will not be requisite that I should examine each in particular, which would be an endless undertaking; for owing to the fact that the destruction of the foundations of necessity brings with it the downfall of the rest of the edifice, I shall only in the first place attack those principles upon which all my former opinions rested.

All that up to the present time I have accepted as most true and certain I have learned either from the senses or through the senses; but it is sometimes proved to me that these senses are deceptive, and it is wiser not to trust entirely to any thing by which we have once been deceived.

But it may be that although the senses sometimes deceive us concerning things which are hardly perceptible, or very far away, there are yet many others to be met with as to which we cannot reasonably have any doubt, although we recognise them by their means. For example, there is the fact that I am here, seated by the fire, attired in a dressing gown, having this paper in my hands and other similar matters. And how could I deny that these hands and this body are mine, were it not perhaps that I compare myself to certain persons, devoid of sense, whose cerebella are so troubled and clouded by the violent vapours of black bile, that they constantly assure us that they think they are kings when they are really quite poor, or that they are clothed in purple when they are really without covering, or who imagine that they have an earthenware head or are nothing but pumpkins or are made of glass. But they are mad, and I should not be any the less insane were I to follow examples so extravagant.

At the same time I must remember that I am a man, and that consequently I am in the habit of sleeping, and in my dreams representing to myself the same things or sometimes even less probable things, than do those who are insane in their waking moments. How often has it happened to me that in the night I

51

Lineage

I honour all who came before,
whose universal wisdom I wore,
who led me through this door.

Mahayana Buddhist studies, practice and refuge as Lobsang Tsundu
at Kopan Monastery, Nepal under the venerable Geshe Lobsang Nyenda.

Vajrana Buddhist studies at The Centre for Gross National Happiness;
Kingdom of Bhutan.

Vipassana Meditation studies and practice under esteemed S.N. Goenka.

Zen and Insight Meditation studies and practice under guru
Gil Fronsdal, Insight Meditation Centre, Redwood City California.

Philosophy and Psychology undergraduate studies at York University.
Meditations under Descartes' scholar Professor Stanley Tweyman.

Mindfulness Certification studies at the University of Toronto
under the direction of bodhisattvas Michele Shaban and Michael Apollo.

Prior works; Time Shift; Managing Time to Create a Life You Love
and 27himalayandays; a Quest for Compassion and Enlightenment.

OTTER Award from the Ontario Society for Training and
Development for executive coaching and development.

Lewis Beaton Scholarship and Alumnus of Distinction
from Durham College of Applied Arts and Technology.

Eric Hoffer International Book Award nomination for poetry
humour and philosophy.

Gratitude

My standing ovation for inspiration,
dedication, insight and talent in this situation.
The universe works through your mind stations.

Cathy Brown for cheerleading.

Barbara Yezik for layout and design.

Grace Thomson and Markelangello for original art.

Donald Robertson HOW TO THINK LIKE A ROMAN EMPEROR, for cover inspiration.

Darren, Sarah, Brent, Michael, Katie, Karen, Colin, Lucinda, Lewis, Lori, Don, Kevin, Diane, Sherry, Kerri, Jane, Mike, Justin, Barb H., Barb Y., Laurisa, Gloria, Debbie, Guy, Jill, Michelle, John, Rhonda, Andre, Louise, Mitch, Nicole, Cindy, Sally, George, Alyson, Steve, Hudson, Colton, Christopher, Allie, Cathy, Wes, Marian, Jackson, Levi, Dustin, Katie, Emma and Harper...Thank you focus friends and family for providing your brilliant gifts. The list is incomplete and the gifts immensely greater, please forgive me for any individual oversight.

Dedication of Merit All merit earned from the production of this book is dedicated to increasing youth philosophy and mindfulness inquiry.